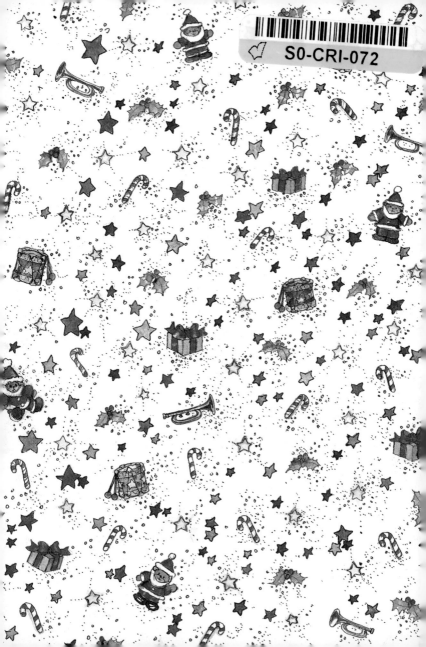

To: Christopher &
Emily

From: GRAN
ADDISON
Dec '98

Clement C. Moore

Illustrated by Lucy Rigg

he C. R. Gibson Company, Norwalk, Ct. 06856

'Twas the night before
Christmas,

when all through the house,

Not a creature was stirring,

not even a mouse.

The stockings were hung

by the chimney with care,

In hopes that St. Nicholas

soon would be there;

TO SANTA
WITH LOVE
FROM ALL
OF US. xxx
°°°°°°°

The children were nestled
all snug in their beds,
While visions of sugar plums
danced in their heads;

And Mama in her 'kerchief,
and I in my cap,
Had just settled down
for a long winter's nap,

When out on the lawn
there arose such a clatter,
I sprang from the bed to see
what was the matter.

Away to the window
I flew like a flash,
Tore open the shutters
and threw up the sash.

The moon on the breast
of the new-fallen snow
Gave a luster of mid-day
to objects below.

When, what to my wondering
eyes should appear,
But a miniature sleigh
and eight tiny reindeer.

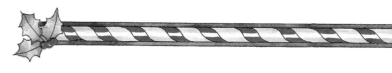

With a little old driver,

so lively and quick,

I knew in a moment

it must be St. Nick.

More rapid than eagles

his coursers they came,

And he whistled, and shouted,

and called them by name:

"Now, Dasher! now, Dancer!
    now, Prancer and Vixen!
On, Comet! on, Cupid!
    on, Donder and Blitzen!

To the top of the porch!
    to the top of the wall!
Now dash away! dash away!
    dash away all!"

As dry leaves that before
the wild hurricane fly,
When they meet with an
obstacle, mount to the sky,

So up to the house-top
the coursers they flew,
With a sleigh full of toys,
and St. Nicholas, too.

LUCY RIGG ©94

And then, in a twinkling,
    I heard on the roof
The prancing and pawing
    of each little hoof.

As I drew in my head,
    and was turning around,
Down the chimney St. Nicholas
    came with a bound.

He was dressed all in fur,
 from his head to his foot,
And his clothes were all tarnished
 with ashes and soot;

A bundle of toys
 he had flung on his back,
And he looked like a peddler
 just opening his pack,

His eyes - how they twinkled!
 his dimples how merry!
His cheeks were like roses,
 his nose like a cherry!

His droll little mouth
    was drawn up like a bow,
And the beard on his chin
    was as white as the snow;

The stump of a pipe
   he held tight in his teeth,
And the smoke, it encircled
   his head like a wreath;

He had a broad face
   and a little round belly
That shook when he laughed,
   like a bowlful of jelly.

He was chubby and plump,
   a right jolly old elf,
And I laughed when I saw him,
   in spite of myself.

A wink of his eye
and a twist of his head,
Soon gave me to know
I had nothing to dread.

He spoke not a word, but
    went straight to his work,
And filled all the stockings;
    then turned with a jerk,

And laying his finger
    aside of his nose,
And giving a nod,
    up the chimney he rose.

He sprang to his sleigh,

   to his team gave a whistle,

And away they all flew

   like the down of a thistle.

But I heard him exclaim,
   ere he drove out of sight,
"Happy Christmas to all,
   and to all a good~night."

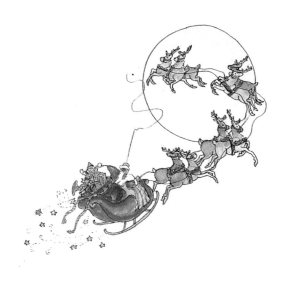

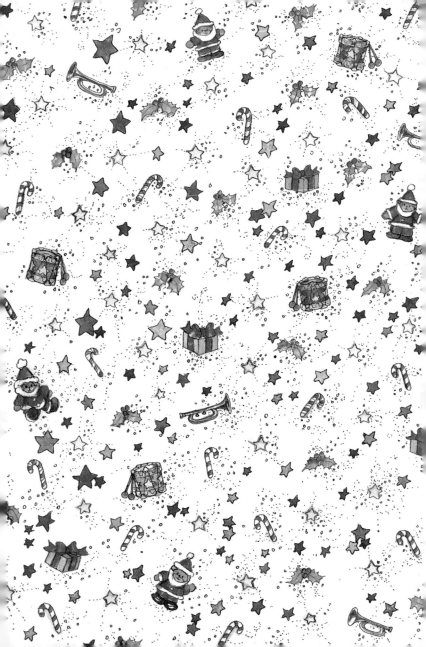